"THE END OF THE TRAIL" • JAMES EARLE FRASER • PLASTER, 1915.

THE VISITOR to the National Cowboy Hall of Fame is greeted by the life-sized statue of a weary cowboy facing the western sunset. This poignant image, "Welcome Sundown," is only one of several monumental art works at the Hall. Upon entering the front doors, "The End of the Trail," a spellbinding sculpture of an exhausted Native American horseman, dominates the space. Later the visitor comes face-to-face with the eighteen foot marble sculpture, "Canyon Princess," which stands as guardian at the art gallery entrance.

Experiencing the beauty of monumental sculpture continues as the visitor tours the gardens behind the museum where "Buffalo Bill" looms large. This entire garden area is a place of natural wonders that delight the eye. The centerpiece of the grounds is the Sutherland Garden with its tinkling waterfall, still ponds, and profusion of natural vegetation. It is complemented by the secluded Atherton Garden and Western States Plaza whose colorful flower beds and sparkling pool accents "The End of the Trail" visible in its glass enclosure.

THE BACK OF THE MUSEUM AS VIEWED FROM THE WESTERN STATES PLAZA.

"THE REMUDA" (TOM RYAN, EIFS, 1996) RUNS THE ENTIRE 350 FOOT LENGTH OF THE HALL'S WEST FACADE.

"Buffalo Bill" (Leonard McMurry, Bronze, 1977) remains the focus of the Hall's garden area.

The Norma Sutherland Garden with its tinkling waterfall, still ponds, and natural vegetation dominates the outdoor spaces between the wings.

The eighteen foot tall "Canyon Princess" (Gerald Balciar, marble, 1995) acts as guardian of the entrance to the art galleries.

JOHN WAYNE, more than any other individual, represents the spirit of the West. The National Cowboy Hall of Fame is proud to perpetuate his legacy in a unique setting that highlights many of the "Duke's" personal possessions. A Raymond Kinstler portrait of Wayne introduces a collection of such diversity that the complex nature of this American hero shines through. But perhaps the most interesting items are from his many movie triumphs. Shown against the backdrop of enlarged photographs from shooting locations, these objects include the famous rifle from "Stagecoach," a Bowie knife from "Alamo," and numerous others. These items form the centerpiece of the Western Entertainment Gallery where the contributions of music, movies, and television to the western entertainment genre are interpreted.

In association with the Wayne collection is a small theater area where clips from his many films run constantly. There the Duke comes alive again at the "Alamo," faces down Liberty Valence in "The Man Who Shot Liberty Valence," and delivers the "writ wrote for a rat" scene from "True Grit." When you leave, you carry good memories of the way life should be.

"JOHN WAYNE" • EVERETT RAYMOND KINSTLER • OIL, 1978.

THE MODEL 92 WINCHESTER MODIFIED FOR THE
MOVIE "STAGECOACH" AND USED THROUGHOUT
JOHN WAYNE'S MOVIE CAREER.

"MANA MAIDEN" HOPI KACHINA DOLL,
JOHN WAYNE COLLECTION.

REVOLVERS USED IN *THE SHOOTIST*, 1951-1962,
JOHN WAYNE COLLECTION.

MUCH OF what we believe about the West, some true and some not so true, revolves around strong images developed on stage and screen. Actors who have contributed to the western genre are annually inducted into the Western Performers Hall of Fame. Recipients of this award range from such early-day movie stars as Gary Cooper to the cast of the contemporary television series, "Little House on the Prairie."

The Western Entertainment Gallery honors the recipients of this award as well as chronicling the development of western entertainment from its beginnings in the wild west shows through modern television dramas. The gallery is filled with fond memories of hours spent in movie theaters or sprawled on the living room couch experiencing the West of the imagination. Things like Gene Autry's guitar, Smiley Burnett's hat, Barbara Stanwyck's familiar black leather costume from "Big Valley," saddles belonging to stars ranging from Tom Mix to Tom Selleck, and a host of other memorabilia evoke nostalgic memories. Walls covered with brightly colored movie posters and paintings of western stars round out a space that tugs at the heart strings of our memory.

"JAMES ARNESS AS MATT DILLON" • JOHN HOWARD SANDEN • OIL, 1981.

"MILBURN STONE AS DOC ADAMS" • ROBERT KUESTER • OIL, 1989.

"ROY ROGERS AND DALE EVANS" • EVERETT RAYMOND KINSTLER • OIL, 1978.

"KEN CURTIS AS FESTUS" • FRANCIS BEAUGUREAU • OIL, 1981.

"GLENN FORD" • J. ANTHONY WILLS • OIL, 1979.

"JAMES STEWART" • ROBERT ABBETT • OIL, 1975.

AN EXAMPLE OF ONE OF
THE SADDLES USED IN
WESTERN MOVIES.

"TOM MIX" • LAJOS MARKOS • OIL, 1977.

"GENE AUTRY" • ROBERT RISHELL • OIL, 1973.

"RANDOLPH SCOTT" • HARLEY BROWN • OIL, 1989.

This replica of a ca. 1860-1870 stock saddle was used by Tom Selleck in his 1997 made for television movie, "Last Stand at Saber River."

Barbara Stanwyck's leather outfit from the "Big Valley" (1965-1969) television series points out the petite size of this legendary actress.

"Barbara Stanwyck" • Bettina Steinke • Oil, 1974.

ALLIED ARTISTS presents

JOEL McCREA

FILMED IN
CINEMASCOPE
COLOR
BY DE LUXE

THE
OKLAHOMAN

BARBARA HALE · BRAD DEXTER · GLORIA TALBOTT with MICHAEL PATE · VERNA FELTON

A WALTER MIRISCH Production · Directed by FRANCIS D. LYON · Written by DANIEL B. ULLMAN

POPULAR WESTERN STAR JOEL McCREA (1905-1990) MADE
"THE OKLAHOMAN" IN 1956.

THE BIG MELO-DRAMATIC MUSICAL SUCCESS

THE COW-BOY GIRL

7 BIG SONG HITS

"FOUR BAD MEN FROM ARIZONA"

"THE COWBOY GIRL" · CA.1910, WAS TYPICAL OF THEATRICAL PLAYS
TOURING SMALL TOWN AMERICA.

A FIRST DIVISION
PRODUCTION

HOOT
GIBSON
IN
"SUNSET RANGE"

SCREEN PLAY BY PAUL SCHOFIELD   DIRECTED BY RAY McCAREY

HOOT GIBSON (1892-1962) WAS ONE OF THE FEW SILENT SCREEN STARS WHO MADE THE TRANSITION TO THE
"TALKIES" AS INDICATED IN THIS 1935 PRODUCTION OF "SUNSET RANGE."

THE CENTRAL character of America's colorful ranching heritage is called a cowboy or vaquero, buckaroo, or drover, depending upon his ancestry and locale. Ranch work required good riding and roping skills. Though daily chores tended to be more mundane than heroic, the cowboy's knowledge and his ability as a horseman set him apart from the miners, farmers, and other laborers on the frontier.

The American Cowboy Gallery looks at the many facets of the cowboy that range from lifestyle to business. Regional variation in gear and costume between northern and southern ranges as well as distinctive elements presented by Black Cowboys, Native American Cowboys, Hispanic Cowboys, and Cowgirls come to life in this presentation. The era of the great cattle drives, complete with a gigantic granite floor map and audio narration on the process provide a fascinating story. Branding and barbed wire overwhelm the visitor with thousands of examples. Luis Ortega's superb rawhide braiding art craft enjoys a complete room. The list goes on and on as it fully explores one of the great stories of a legendary way-of-life.

THE CHUCK WAGON SERVED AS A MOBILE KITCHEN FOR COWBOYS DURING ROUNDUP OR ON TRAIL DRIVES.

A VAQUERO ROLLS UP HIS "SOOGANS" (BEDROLL) BEFORE STARTING HIS DAYS WORK.

AN IMPORTANT PART OF ANY TRAIL DRIVE OR ROUNDUP WAS THE CAMP WHERE THE CHUCK WAGON STAYED, "COOKIE" PREPARED MEALS, AND THE COWBOYS SLEPT.

THIS ROOM IS DEDICATED TO RANCHING TRADITIONS AND IT CHRONICLES THE HISTORY OF RANCHING IN AMERICA FROM ITS HISPANIC ORIGINS TO THE PRESENT.

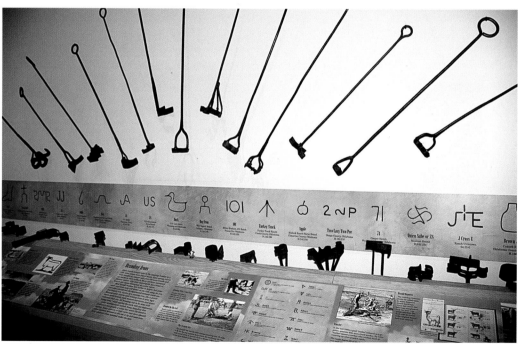

BRANDING IRONS MARKED CATTLE OWNERSHIP AND BARBED WIRE KEPT THE LIVESTOCK IN THEIR PROPER PASTURES AS ILLUSTRATED BY ALMOST 2000 EXAMPLES IN THIS EXHIBIT.

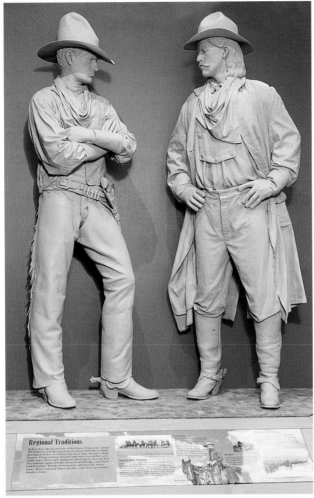

A SOUTHERN PLAINS COWBOY AND A NORTHERN PLAINS COWBOY SIZE EACH OTHER UP IN A VIGNETTE THAT ILLUSTRATES REGIONAL DIFFERENCE IN COWBOY COSTUME.

THE COWGIRL DRESSED IN HER DISTINCTIVE RIDING OUTFIT IS CLEARLY ILLUSTRATED IN THIS POSE.

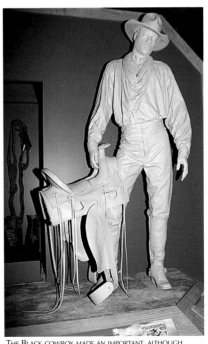

THE BLACK COWBOY MADE AN IMPORTANT, ALTHOUGH LARGELY OVERLOOKED, CONTRIBUTION TO THE COWBOY WAY-OF-LIFE IN THE 19TH CENTURY.

THIS TYPICAL BUNKHOUSE OF THE 1880 PERIOD HOUSES ALL THE PERSONAL POSSESSIONS OF THE COWBOY AND ILLUSTRATES HIS LIFESTYLE.

"DUSTY TRAILS AND DRY CAMP" • JOE GRANDEE • OIL, 1996 • ADORNS THE WALL IN THE TRAIL DRIVE AREA.

A VIGNETTE OF AN 18TH CENTURY CALIFORNIA VAQUERO EPITOMIZES THE HISPANIC ORIGINS OF RANCHING IN AMERICA.

THE CHARRO COSTUME OF MEXICO PROVIDES ANOTHER GLIMPSE OF HISPANIC RANCHING INFLUENCE IN THE AMERICAS.

RODEO CONJURES up exciting images of riding and roping contests where bucking horses, bad Brahma bulls, and all the fast moving action of America's only indigenous sport rules the day. All that and more appear in the American Rodeo Gallery where you enter a 1950s rodeo arena bursting with all the sights and sounds of a performance in progress.

Within the arena are six fascinating presentations illustrating the six major rodeo events. Meanwhile, a movie history of rodeo, narrated by entertainer Reba McEntire and rodeo announcer Clem McSpadden, plays before the arena bleachers. For those interested in the heros and champions of the sport, a touch screen computer provides biographies and images of favorite performers. The "Eyes on the Prize" portion of the area is replete with silver trophies and unbelievably ornate championship buckles won since the turn of the century. Additionally, a host of memorabilia filled cases trace the history of rodeo complete with women's roles and spotlighting subsidiary activities such as clowns and trick riding and roping. The American Rodeo Gallery is indeed one of those once-in-a-lifetime experiences.

A LIFE-SIZE SCULPTURE OF THE GREAT RODEO PERFORMER, BILL LINDERMAN, WELCOMES VISITORS AT THE ENTRANCE OF THE AMERICAN RODEO GALLERY.

"ROY COOPER" • WILLIAM F. DRAPER • OIL, 1983.

A LIFELIKE BUCKING SADDLE BRONC AND RIDER PROVIDES A TOUCH OF EXCITEMENT TO THE RODEO ARENA AREA.

"PAUL TIERNEY" • RICHARD WILEY • OIL, 1981.

"JIM SHOULDERS" • CHARLES BANKS WILSON • OIL, 1979.

"BILL SMITH" • JAMES BAMA • OIL, 1974.

*The first formal rodeo is
thought to have been held
in 1888 in Prescott, Arizona,
a claim disputed by Pecos,
Texas and Denver, Colorado.*

"LEO CAMARILLO" • FRANCIS BEAUGUREAU • OIL, 1976.

"CHRIS LYBBERT" • ROBERT SKEMP • OIL, 1983.

"DEAN OLIVER" • FRANCIS BEAUGUREAU • OIL, 1978.

"JIMMY COOPER" • JOHN H. SANDEN • OIL, 1981.

"CASEY TIBBS" • FRANCIS BEAUGUREAU • OIL, 1981.

"EVERETT SHAW" • EVERETT RAYMOND KINSTLER • OIL, 1980.

THIS 9TH CAVALRY OR "BUFFALO SOLDIER" BUGLER IN FULL REGALIA STANDS AS THE CENTERPIECE OF THE FRONTIER MILITARY PRESENTATION.

EXPERIENCE THE exciting history of the frontier West via the fabulous Joe Grandee collection acquired by the Hall several years ago. Here, for the first time, the marvelous objects of that assemblage are shown together. They tell the story of the fur trade, Native American lifestyle, military activities on the frontier, and hunting in the West in a way that has never been done before.

A giant photographic panorama of western landscape greets the visitor upon entering the gallery. That is quickly supplanted by the fur trade exhibit where Hawken rifles, Hudson Bay blankets, and other gear tell the colorful story of the mountain men. Adjacent to that is an area dedicated to the Plains Indian horse culture which emphasizes the extreme mobility of those people through their personal effects that are adapted to a nomadic lifestyle. One of the larger areas in the Grandee Gallery is dedicated to the military on the frontier where lifestyle, campaigns, barracks life, and the various branches of the service are clearly illustrated. Yet another major space involves hunting, both for sport and for profit, in the West where numerous artifacts are complemented by outstanding dioramas of hunting scenes.

THE BUFFALO STAND SHOOT DIORAMA THAT DOMINATES THE "HUNTING IN THE WEST" AREA PRESENTS AN OUTSTANDINGLY ACCURATE DEPICTION OF A NINETEENTH CENTURY COMMERCIAL HUNTING TECHNIQUE.

WESTERN ART comprises a significant part of the National Cowboy Hall of Fame's presentation. Major works produced from the early nineteenth century to the present adorn the Hall's permanent galleries. In addition, the museum maintains changing art exhibits both from its own collection and borrowed from other institutions. Thus, a varied menu of fine western art is always on display.

The permanent art collection contains works from Charles M. Russell and Frederic Remington, both considered masters of the genre. Additionally, there are selections from the Taos school, including works by Walter Ufer, Joseph Sharp, Nicolai Fechin, and others. Individual artists include N.C. Wyeth, Frank Tenney Johnson, William R. Leigh and many more of the same caliber. Contemporary western artists are represented by masters of the craft like Wilson Hurley, Tom Lovell, James Reynolds, Bob Kuhn, and Tucker Smith to name only a few.

The Hall also has an immense collection of Native American art displayed on a rotating basis. These works include early ledger book art, pieces from the Kiowa Five, selections from the Bacone School, art from the Santa Fe School, and a host of material from individual artists.

"EMIGRANTS CROSSING THE PLAINS" • ALBERT BIERSTADT • OIL, 1867.

"Target Practice" • Tom Lovell • Oil, 1986.

"Sharing an Apple" • Tom Ryan • Oil, 1969.

"Bell Remuda" • Robert Lougheed • Oil, 1969.

"The Return of Summer" • Tucker Smith • Oil, 1990.

"Arizona Cowboys" • James E. Reynolds • Oil, 1992.

"ROUGH RIDING RANCHEROS" • FRANK TENNEY JOHNSON • OIL, 1935.

"LEWIS AND CLARK WITH SACAJAWEA" •
HENRY LION • BRONZE, UNKNOWN.

"THE ADMIRABLE OUTLAW" • NEWELL C. WYETH • OIL, 1906.

"SAND PAINTER" • E.I. COUSE • OIL, 1927.

"PUEBLO RIDER" • AWA TSIREH • GOUACHE ON PAPER, CA. 1920.

"CHEYENNE IN THE MOON" • BENNIE BUFFALO • LITHOGRAPH ON PAPER, 1991.

In 1880, at the tender age of sixteen, Charles Marion Russell left his comfortable Saint Louis home for a cowboy's life in Montana Territory. There he stayed and there he became a legend by painting and creating sculptures of his beloved western lifestyle "up close and personal." His was a labor of love and our lives are richer for it.

The C.M. Russell art at the National Cowboy Hall of Fame include "Smoke Talk" and "Red Man's Wireless," both excellent examples of his Native American images. "Red Man's Wireless" particularly illustrates Russell's use of intense color to bring his imagery to life. Other paintings such as "Wildman's Truce" and "Before the White Man Came" show an Indian lifestyle that fascinated the artist who was much admired by the Native Americans of Montana.

Russell's other fascination, cowboys and western lifestyle, appear in a variety of works. "When Mules Wear Diamonds" provides a vivid depiction of the rugged work of packing in the mountains. "The Whiskey Smugglers" and "Caught in the Circle" are action packed scenes of lawlessness and warfare. Finally, nostalgia for a time gone by shines through in "When Wagon Trails Were Dim." Charlie's art tells tales, much like the yarns the artist himself spun, of a time past in need of being remembered.

"Wildman's Truce" • C.M. Russell • Oil, 1914.

"Buffalo Hunt" • C.M. Russell • Bronze, 1905.

"Planning the Attack" • C.M. Russell • Oil, 1900.

"Smoke Talk" • C.M. Russell • Oil, 1924.

"Before the White Man Came" • C.M. Russell • Oil, 1897.

"RED MAN'S WIRELESS" • C.M. RUSSELL • OIL, 1916.

"CALL OF THE LAW" • C.M. RUSSELL • OIL, 1911.

THE WEST captivated Frederic Remington's imagination from his earliest visit in 1881 until his death in 1909. First as a magazine illustrator and later as a painter and sculptor, his images remain the best known of the western genre. "Hunters Camp in the Big Horn" and "In From the Night Herd" are among the Remington paintings on display at the Hall. But his best known work, a statue of four cowboys riding recklessly across the plains, entitled "Coming Through the Rye" along with "The Bronco Buster," "The Mountain Man," and many others are on display at the National Cowboy Hall of Fame.

"LIN McLEAN" • FREDERIC REMINGTON • WATERCOLOR, 1897.

"THE BRONCO BUSTER" • FREDERIC REMINGTON • BRONZE, 1917.

"HUNTERS CAMP ON THE BIGHORN" • FREDERIC REMINGTON • OIL, 1909.

"THE MOUNTAIN MAN" • FREDERIC REMINGTON • BRONZE, 1918.

Welcome to "Prosperity Junction," our turn-of-the-century cattle town, where you are transported back to another era where time freezes at twilight and where the streets have the golden glow of light cascading from doors and windows. The sound of the prairie wind, of a passing horse and rider, the distant mournful strains of a train whistle, and other everyday noises surround your trip to the past. As you stroll down Main Street you hear lively rinky tink piano music at the saloon and, further along, the peaceful sounds of organ music at the open doors of the church. All this transpires in a setting that suspends the visitor at another time in another place.

Enter the buildings and enjoy the ambiance of a more relaxed time. All of the structures are filled with objects dating from the turn of the century. You can visit the saddle shop, blacksmith, and train depot at one end of town, the church and school at the other, or maybe some of the many businesses in between. Regardless of the length of your stay in "Prosperity Junction," your visit will be a pleasant and memorable experience.

ENTRANCE INTO "PROSPERITY JUNCTION," WHERE YOU RETURN TO ANOTHER CENTURY, IS MADE THROUGH THE LIVERY STABLE.

THIS ORIGINAL CONCORD STAGECOACH, CA. 1880, STAYS IN THE LIVERY STABLE READY TO MAKE ITS DAILY RUN FOR THE LEE WAY COACH COMPANY.

HORSES IN THEIR STALLS, LUGGAGE READY TO LOAD ON THE COACH, AND THE STAGECOACH ITSELF, PUT UP FOR THE NIGHT ALONG WITH ITS ASSOCIATED EQUIPMENT, MAKE UP THE SETTING FOR THE LIVERY STABLE.

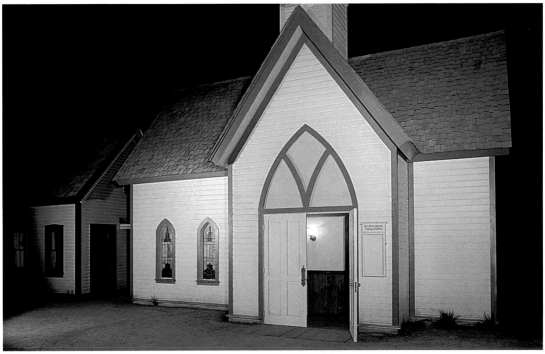

"PROSPERITY JUNCTION'S" PLACE OF WORSHIP IS A REPLICA OF A SMALL TOWN CHURCH IN THE WEST.

THE INTERIOR OF THE CHURCH IS FULLY FURNISHED WITH SMALL SIZED PEWS, A PULPIT, AND AN ORGAN PLAYING FAMILIAR HYMNS THAT LENDS AN AIR OF PEACE AND TRANQUILITY TO THE SCENE.

THE CHURCH DOMINATES THE SOUTH END OF MAIN STREET.

THE NORTH END OF MAIN STREET IS BLOCKED BY CATTLE CAR, WHICH IS FLANKED ON ONE SIDE BY THE TRAIN DEPOT AND ON THE OTHER BY THE EXPRESS LAND AND CATTLE COMPANY.

THE UNION PACIFIC DEPOT IN "PROSPERITY JUNCTION" STILL SPORTS THE TOWN'S ORIGINAL NAME OF "PROSPERITY."

RULES FOR RIDING THE STAGECOACH AND A SCHEDULE OF ARRIVALS AND DEPARTURES ARE PROMINENTLY POSTED IN THE LIVERY STABLE.

The Cattlemen's State Bank dominates the corner of Main and Oak on the south end of town.

Furnishings for the bank are original 1901 fixtures from the Hunter, Oklahoma Bank that closed in the 1980s.

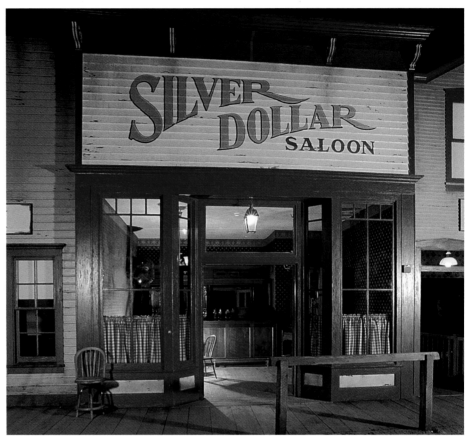

The "Silver Dollar Saloon" is typical of its day where swinging "bat wing" doors, so popularized by the movies, were as scarce as hen's teeth, but where free lunch was offered to those buying drinks.

Inside the "Silver Dollar" a player piano blasts out period music, while the bar stands ready to serve a thirsty clientele.

IN ADDITION TO PROVIDING ANY MERCHANDISE THE TOWNSFOLK MIGHT NEED, THE MERCANTILE ALSO SERVES AS THE COMMUNITY POST OFFICE.

"FLEMING MERCANTILE," WITH ITS SUBSTANTIAL BRICK CONSTRUCTION AND LIVING QUARTERS ON THE SECOND FLOOR IS THE MOST SUCCESSFUL BUSINESS IN TOWN.

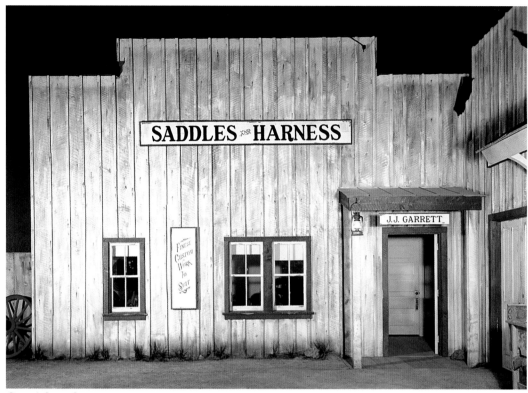

GARRETT'S SADDLE SHOP AND ITS ASSOCIATED SHOWROOM ILLUSTRATES THE IMPORTANCE OF HORSES AT THE TURN OF THE CENTURY.

THE BLACKSMITH SHOP, WITH ITS GLOWING FORGE, ARRAY OF TOOLS, AND RINGING SOUND OF HAMMER ON STEEL REMAINS AN INDISPENSABLE PART OF A TOWN DEPENDENT ON HORSES FOR TRANSPORTATION.

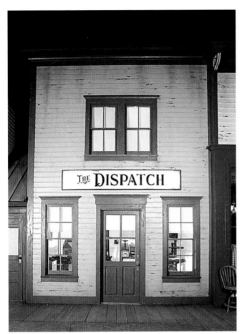

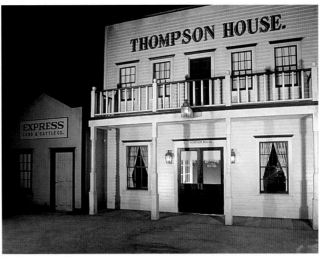

THE "THOMPSON HOUSE" HOTEL HAS JUST BEEN REFURBISHED AND PROVIDES FOOD AND LODGING TO THOSE ARRIVING IN TOWN BY RAIL.

THE PROSPERITY JUNCTION "DISPATCH" IS THE MAIN BOOSTER OF THE COMMUNITY, AND FREE COPIES OF ITS LATEST EDITION ARE TO BE FOUND AT NEWSSTANDS ALONG MAIN STREET.

ACTUAL CLASSES ARE TAUGHT IN THE SCHOOL USING BOOKS, SLATES, AND TECHNIQUES COMMON TO THE 1890-1900 ERA.

CHILDREN'S COWBOY CORRAL

THE CHILDREN'S Cowboy Corral remains one of the most popular areas at the Hall. It is a children's museum where youngsters of all ages can experience being a cowboy through a variety of interactive experiences. Instead of just looking at "stuff," they get to play with "stuff."

When visitors enter the area they are greeted by a cowboy mannequin who explains various aspects of cowboy life through songs, stories, and simple explanations. Then there are the saddles where the little buckaroos can mount up and pretend to ride or, if they prefer high tech, play a computer game about cowboy life. But maybe the most popular area is the bunkhouse where little guys, and sometimes grownups if nobody is watching, can try on cowboy boots, spurs, chaps, vests, and other gear and usually get their pictures taken in the process. Then, of course, they can play around the chuck wagon, check out the longhorn steer, and, in general, have a rip-roaring good time playing out a fantasy. Time spent at the CCC Ranch, as it is sometimes called, is a real learning experience that young and old alike will remember for years to come.

TRYING ON REAL COWBOY BOOTS.

PRETENDING TO BE ON A BUCKING BRONCO.

RIDING THE RANGE.

Up close and personal, a longhorn steer is really big.

Learning from the singing cowboy.

Camping out during roundup looks like fun.

Trying to get fed at the chuck wagon.

EDUCATION IS an important aspect of the National Cowboy Hall of Fame. As a museum, the Hall is able to serve a wide variety of students ranging in age from four to eighty-four. Regular classroom and gallery sessions are conducted for area schools, while a schedule of evening adult classes cover a wide range of western subjects. Each year the Hall sponsors four week-long art schools conducted by award-winning professional artists, and throughout the year a variety of other educational opportunities are offered. Additionally, seminars and other social programs are offered in conjunction with the museum's changing exhibition schedule.

The education program is underpinned by a significant research center that can be used by the public by appointment only. This library and archive contains hundreds of thousands of photographs, documents, videos, and archival materials as well as over 50,000 books supporting the subject matter of the museum.

Meanwhile, "Trappings of the West," the Hall's museum store, offers a wide variety of books for sale on western topics that elaborate on exhibition subjects. Naturally, the store also contains a variety of other items that appeal to shoppers who enjoy merchandise with a western flair.

CHILDREN'S CLASSROOM PRESENTATIONS ARE AVAILABLE THROUGHOUT THE YEAR.

ART DEMONSTRATIONS DOMINATE PRIX DE WEST ACTIVITIES DURING THE SECOND WEEKEND IN JUNE OF EACH YEAR.

THE READING ROOM OF THE RESEARCH CENTER IS DEVOTED TO THE SERIOUS STUDY OF WESTERN HISTORY.

THE RESEARCH CENTER CONTAINS ROWS AND ROWS OF BOOKS, PHOTO CABINETS, VIDEO SHELVES, AND OTHER MATERIALS, ALL DEVOTED TO THE STUDY OF THE AMERICAN WEST.

WEEK-LONG ART CLASSES BY PROMINENT PRIX DE WEST ARTISTS ARE PRESENTED FOUR TIMES EACH YEAR.

THE PLEASANTLY ARRANGED MUSEUM STORE AT THE HALL PROVIDES EVERYTHING THE MUSEUM SHOPPER MIGHT WANT.

A FULL range of activities, from family oriented happenings to very exclusive formal events, occur at the National Cowboy Hall of Fame. Not a month passes without some outstanding program being made available to the public. Somewhere in this mix is something for you.

A partial listing includes:

January: **Spring Exhibition Opening** (LEARNING - FUN)

February: **Dinner Theater** (ONE MAN SHOW - WESTERN THEME - FUN)

March: **Cowboy Poetry Gathering** (50 PERFORMERS - COMEDY - PATHOS - MUSIC - FUN)

April: **Western Heritage Awards** (MOVIE STARS - MUSICIANS - AUTHORS - CELEBRITIES - FUN)

May: **Chuckwagon Gathering and Children's Cowboy Festival** (FOOD - MUSIC - RIDES - GAMES - FUN)

June: **Prix de West Art Exhibition and Sale** (ARTISTS - SEMINARS - FOOD - FUN)

July: **Children's Art Classes** (ART - LEARNING - FUN)

August: **Adult Art Classes** (ART - LEARNING - FUN)

September: **Fall Exhibition Opening** (LEARNING - FUN)

October: **Rodeo Historical Society Induction Weekend** (RODEO CHAMPIONS - WESTERN DANCE - FUN)

November: **Adult Art Classes** (ART - LEARNING - FUN)

December: **Two Weeks of Christmas Celebration** (CHOIRS - FOOD - COWBOY CHRISTMAS BALL - FUN).

COME - VISIT - ENJOY

NATIVE AMERICAN EDUCATION PROGRAM.

"CHUCKWAGON GATHERING" FOOD PREPARATION.

"Medicine Show" fun at the "Chuckwagon Gathering."

Stage entertainment takes place at most hall events.

Formal events like "Western Heritage Awards" fill the "Noble Special Events Center" with an array of celebrities and entertainers.

OPENED IN the winter of 1994, the Sam Noble Special Events center represents one of the newest additions to the Hall. Its 16,000 square foot space is home to five of the most spectacular triptych landscapes ever done on the west. Each of these pieces stretch 46 feet long by 18 feet high. Four of them reside in the corners of the room and one is centered on the back wall, so that the room is surrounded by the beauty of the west.

Premier western landscapist, Wilson Hurley of Albuquerque, New Mexico, painted these "windows on the west." They are specifically designed for the room with the sun setting in the west and the remaining images receiving light on the same horizon line from that sunset. "California Suite," sunset over the Pacific at Point Lobos, is the first window followed by "Arizona Suite," a view of the Grand Canyon from an unusual lower level looking upward. The "New Mexico Suite" allows the viewer to experience an apocalyptic sky over the Sandia Mountains from the west side of the Rio Grande near Albuquerque while "Utah Suite" catches a cloudless sky over Monument Valley. The last of the windows, "Wyoming Suite," is a spectacular image of the Lower Falls of the Yellowstone seen from below and looking upward through the pines.

"UTAH SUITE" • WILSON HURLEY • OIL, 1995.

"NEW MEXICO SUITE" • WILSON HURLEY • OIL, 1992.

"CALIFORNIA SUITE" • WILSON HURLEY • OIL, 1994.